PRELUDE

In folklore, angels tickle harps and the Devil plays
the violin. So it is hardly surprising
that extraordinary musical
ability in mere mortals has
long been explained
by way of heaven-
ly blessings or, more
frequently, dark pacts. Two cen-
turies before Robert Johnson wielded a
guitar pick, before Jimi Hendrix plugged in his
amplifier, there lived another seemingly super-
human artist of strings, a bolt of lightning
who could fiddle like no one on Earth, a
violinist named Paganini....

For Mom—A.F.

In memory of my grandfather, the occasional fiddler—G.K.

Text copyright © 2008 Aaron Frisch

Illustrations copyright © 2008 Gary Kelley

Published in 2008 by Creative Editions

P.O. Box 227, Mankato, MN 56002 USA

Creative Editions is an imprint of The Creative Company.

Design by Rita Marshall

Printed in Italy

Library of Congress Cataloging-in-Publication Data

Frisch, Aaron.

Dark fiddler: the life and legend of Nicolo Paganini /
by Aaron Frisch; illustrated by Gary Kelley.

ISBN 978-1-56846-200-4

1. Paganini, Nicolo, 1782–1840—Juvenile literature.

2. Violinists—Italy—Biography—Juvenile literature.

3. Composers—Italy—Biography—Juvenile literature. I. Title.

ML3930.P2F75 2008

787.2092—dc22 [B]   2007027412

First edition

9 8 7 6 5 4 3 2 1

DARK FIDDLER

THE LIFE AND LEGEND OF NICOLO PAGANINI

AARON FRISCH

illustrated by
GARY KELLEY

Creative Editions

Old Jacopo stuck his spade into the earth and looked around for Francesco, his young assistant. The boy stood before a marble monument.

"Nicolo Paganini," Francesco read. "So he lived. From the talk, I had thought he was myth."

"The man was real," Jacopo said, "but myth always walked a step behind him." He removed his hat and leaned against a nearby tombstone. There was much work to be done in Parma's gray cemetery, but it could wait for a few minutes.

"Sit," said Jacopo to young Francesco. "Listen, and I will tell you the tale. It ends in the ground before you, but it begins with an angel...."

NICOLO PAGANINI 1782–1840

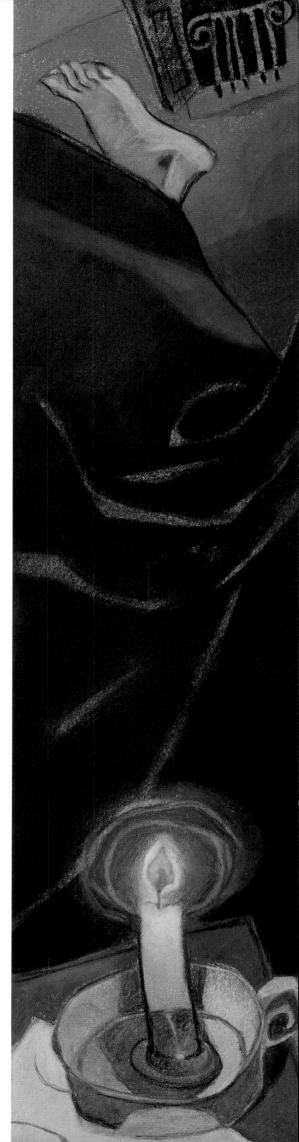

LEGENDS hold that one autumn night near All Hallows' Eve, a winged messenger came by dream to Teresa Paganini, a young Genoese woman heavy with child. "You will bear a son the world will remember," the angel said, "but his fame will not be without cost." Signora Paganini gave birth to a boy named Nicolo.

When Nicolo died of the spotted plague almost before he could speak, the cost seemed steep indeed, and much too soon. But, somehow, he returned from the dead. The boy was shrouded and shovels were brought forth before a mourner saw faint breath. After several winters more, his father Antonio, with visions of wealth, pressed the violin into Nicolo's hands. "No practice, no supper!" Antonio would bellow. And so little Nicolo, skinny and sickly, learned to tune strings and play double stops while other boys watched ships and played in the streets.

Nicolo was special from the start, composing by eight, in concert by nine. Too special. The greatest violinists from his corner of Italy were paid to tutor him, but he outpaced them. So Nicolo trained himself. From dawn to dusk, he found new ways of bouncing bows and plucking strings. Folks in Genoa began to whisper, crossing themselves when the boy brushed past. By fifteen, Nicolo was without peer in all of Italy. At sixteen, he took to the road.

Nicolo's recitals swelled his reputation and means, and he fell fast for wine, games of chance, and pretty ladies. The lad was blown this way and that, losing small fortunes and even his violin to unlucky rolls of dice. His ruin seemed certain. And then, at nineteen, he vanished, into the villa of a mysterious countess, the hearsay goes. For four years, he was seen no more. A new century unfolded. The whispers grew.

Nicolo reemerged at last, more discreet, more gifted, becoming court violinist for Emperor Napoleon's sister. And again he toured. Up, down, and across Italy he went, causing wide eyes and nervous murmurs. Word spread that he could play twelve notes a second. Twelve notes! He did away with sheet music too, putting keys and cadenzas to memory—a thing unheard of. For twenty years, he fiddled from Rome to the smallest hilltowns.

I have spoken of Nicolo's sickly nature, and sick he was for most of his days. Yet even in this he seemed curiously blessed. One disease left his joints too loose, permitting his fingers to stretch and wrists to bend in ways most unnatural. To see him play was half magic, half madness. His bow hand would sweep and slash while the fingers of his left danced and leapt over the strings like a spider chased by fire. Often he would snip three wires from his violin, then offer up a masterpiece on the one that remained.

He would have been a marvel to behold by technique alone, but the music—Saint Cecilia, the music! Songs of his own design, caprices and concertos so complex that he alone in this world could play them. One moment, strapping men wept from the tender beauty of it all. The next, women shrieked and fainted from the ferocity and terrible speed. It was as if Nicolo turned from sunrise to storm before their very eyes.

And oh, the look of him. Gaunt and spindly he was, draped all in black, with skin the color of the moon. Like something made to frighten crows from a vineyard. He had an eerie walk, as if the breeze carried him. He would shake aside his dark mane, roll his eyes to white, and pull from those strings sounds never heard before.

So they thought him some manner of ghoul, or at least on a winking basis with the darkest fiddler of them all. But Nicolo did not fret. He loved it, truth be told, for it made him all the more famous. I always imagined that he grinned a toothless grin—did I mention all his teeth dropped out?—when black steeds sped his carriage from a concert house, leaving bedlam in his wake.

Those closest to him said he ate little and slept much. That he was jealous with his secrets and hard to know. Liable to juggle grapes one moment and gaze glumly upon them the next. Greedy at night and generous by morning. It was as if he were being pulled at from two ends, they said.

Those who knew the man from afar spoke of different things. They said he had learned the craft in a dungeon. That if you looked at just the right moment, you could see the Devil himself guiding Nicolo's elbow. When he set to wider travel, the rumors went that he reached foreign shores on the deck of the *Flying Dutchman*, that awful ghost ship. One story topped another. Little wonder crowds took to poking him with canes to see if he were blood and bone.

At last, four decades along, Nicolo embarked on the tour of

tours. In five years' time, he put Europe under his spell.

Austria. Germany. France. England. In Vienna, the commotion

was beyond words, his name bandied in the streets, his likeness

painted on storefronts, his melodies whistled in courtyards. In

Germany, he enchanted the masses by humoring their local

bowmen in fiddling duels. Everywhere, concert houses over-

filled two hours before a note was played.

The French told and retold the tale of Nicolo's impromptu

charity concert for a young maid in need, performing on her

wooden shoe, which he had strung as a fiddle. The British

were every bit as enthralled, trailing him like shadows in

hopes of uncloaking his tricks. Liszt, Chopin, Schumann—all the

giants of music came out to see him. The whispers that had

taken seed so many years before bloomed into applause that

seemed never to end.

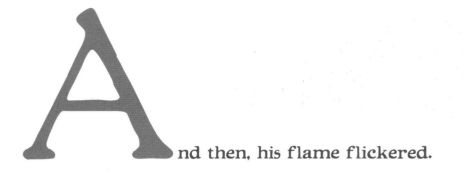nd then, his flame flickered.

Bad health, you see.

He returned home and appeared less and less. I saw him play myself once, in 1835, there near the end when he was stooped and worn. I was but a boy, but the sounds I heard that day have never left my ears. He tried then to undo the midnight stories, but it was much too late for that. His hope for a brighter legacy, a great "Casino Paganini" of music and games in Paris, failed, and his strength with it. He died in Nice, fifty-seven years old, arms about his favorite violin.

Nicolo declined the Church's final rites, and half a decade passed before he was allowed into sacred ground. Some say he wasn't fit to rest among the righteous. Some say he isn't among the righteous, buried here or no. Alive or dead he was called many things, but I like to think he was something wholly original. A creature born to put bow to string.

NICOLO PAGANINI 1782-1840

Old Jacopo's story was at an end. A cool breeze crept through the Cemetery della Villetta. Young Francesco's shadow fell on the monument before him.

"I don't know," the boy finally said. "That sounds like a fable to me."

Jacopo rose, using his shovel as a crutch. There were graves to be dug before the sun went down. "Believe as you will," he said, and walked away.

Francesco looked at the stone. A blackbird called out. The boy pulled his hat down tight and hurried after the old man.

POSTLUDE

THE BEGINNING

Nicolo Paganini (*nee-koh-LOH pah-gah-NEE-nee*) was born on October 27, 1782. At the age of four, he was pronounced dead of measles and nearly buried before the error was discovered. Much of his childhood thereafter was spent with a stringed instrument in his hands. Nicolo was a featured performer in churches and local theaters before reaching his teens. By thirteen, he was hailed as a virtuoso, a prodigy of such talent that people alternately spoke of him as a "wonder-child" and a "witch's brat."

BLOOD

Nicolo was among six children born to Teresa and Antonio Paganini. Teresa was a gentle, religious woman, whereas Antonio was a taskmaster, a shipping clerk and mediocre mandolin and violin player who forced music upon his youngest son. Nicolo was happy to leave his father at sixteen but remained close with the rest of his family. Nicolo never married but in 1825 had a son named Achille by singer Antonia Bianchi. He doted on Achille all his life.

THE MUSIC

Nicolo began composing very young after realizing that showcasing his talent would require complex music. From his quill came six violin concertos (solo pieces performed with orchestras) and a more famous set of twenty-four unaccompanied caprices, the last of which—the dazzlingly difficult Caprice No. 24 in A Minor—is considered his greatest achievement. His compositions range from soft, poetic melodies to furious, thrilling works and are still used as a measuring stick in identifying virtuosos.

THE SECRETS

Nicolo's secrets with a violin at his chin were numerous. Many can be explained only by rare physical traits and sheer genius. The uncommon flexibility of his joints let him cover an impossible three octaves in a single hand span, and he showed a staggering gift for improvisation. He also developed the technique of deliberately mistuning strings to create unique sounds and play in different keys, and although many accounts state he rarely rehearsed after his thirtieth birthday, he practiced ferociously—up to fifteen hours a day—behind closed doors during his formative years.

THE ROAD

Aside from his famed European tour of 1828 to 1833, Nicolo did not stray much from his native Italy. He was born in the northwestern port city of Genoa, studied in nearby Parma as a young teen, and at sixteen broke through as a national sensation at Lucca, a Tuscan city where he would be headquartered for a time. He retired to Parma in 1834 after years of touring but soon moved west to Nice, France, in unfulfilled hopes the coastal climate would improve his failing health.

INFLUENCE

Nicolo's exploits and innovations helped plot a course for the careers of many of nineteenth-century Europe's greatest musicians. Polish composer Frédéric Chopin witnessed an 1829 Paganini concert in Warsaw and promptly wrote the piano solo *Souvenir de Paganini*. German pianist Robert Schumann decided to devote his life to music after hearing Nicolo play in Frankfurt. And an 1831 Paganini performance in Paris caused Hungarian pianist Franz Liszt to exclaim, "What a man! What an artist! Heavens! What sufferings, what misery, what torture in those four strings!"

THE END

On his deathbed on May 27, 1840, Nicolo declined his last rites from a priest. Many say he refused to believe he was dying; others proffer a darker explanation. The Church, in turn, denied him proper burial for five years. In death, the violinist seemed to take on a morbid new life, as his body was reburied no fewer than three times in his adopted hometown of Parma between 1876 and 1896. Rumors still swirl as to the final destination of his soul.

SELECTED BIBLIOGRAPHY

De Courcy, G. I. C. *Paganini: The Genoese*. 2 vols. Norman, Okla.: University of Oklahoma Press, 1957.

Pulver, Jeffrey. *Paganini: The Romantic Virtuoso*. New York: Da Capo Press, 1970. First published 1936 by Herbert Joseph, Ltd., London.

Sachs, Harvey. *Virtuoso*. New York: Thames and Hudson, 1982.

Schwarz, Boris. *Great Masters of the Violin*. New York: Simon and Schuster, 1983.

Sheppard, Leslie, and Herbert R. Axelrod. *Paganini*. Neptune, N.J.: Paganiniana Pub., 1979.

Stratton, Stephen S. *Nicolo Paganini: His Life and Work*. Westport, Conn.: Greenwood Press, 1971. First published 1907 by The Strad Office, London, and Charles Scribner's Sons, New York.